BRITAIN IN OLD PHOTOGRAPHS

BACK TO THE
BROADS

DAVID HOLMES

First published in 1998 by Sutton Publishing Limited

This edition published in 2001 by
Lucas Books

Copyright © David Holmes, 1998

Title page photograph: Potter Heigham Staithe, *c*. 1900.

A catalogue record for this book is available from the British Library.

ISBN 0-7509-1790-3

Typeset in 10/12 Perpetua.
Typesetting and origination by
Sutton Publishing Limited.
Printed in Great Britain by
J.H. Haynes & Co. Ltd, Sparkford.

*This book is dedicated
to the memory of
Joan Caroline Lynde (née Boardman)
1902–1998*

Whiteslea Lodge, Lord Desborough's shooting box at Hickling, Easter 1931. Renovations were in progress including the replacement of a tiled roof with thatch.

CONTENTS

The ferryman at Horning, *c.* 1898.

Dick Browne, gamekeeper at Ranworth, *c.* 1950.

INTRODUCTION

B ack to the Broads represents a second selection of photographs, following on from *The Norfolk Broads in Old Photographs*, published in 1996. The story of the Broads has so many facets that it was a challenge deciding what to leave out of the first volume: some of the more obvious omissions have been covered this time. In particular it has been possible in this book to cross the River Waveney and explore that part of Broadland which lies in Suffolk.

The first chapter takes a look at the Norfolk wherry. Although the first trading wherries appeared in the mid-eighteenth century, when they began to take over from the larger, less manoeuvrable keels, the most famous of all wherries celebrates her centenary in 1998. The *Albion*, kept afloat by the efforts of the Norfolk Wherry Trust and kept in good heart by the hard work of craftsmen like Ludham boat builder Mike Fuller, is still a familiar sight on our rivers. The *Maud*, virtually rebuilt by the Pargeter family at Upton, should join her soon. However, the most comfortable and stylish way to enjoy wherrying is aboard the pleasure wherry *Hathor* (built in 1905) or the wherry yachts *Olive* (1909) and *Norada* (1912). Peter Bower, who has taken these three elegant craft into every part of Broadland, knows everything there is to know about wherrying. A cruise with Wherry Yacht Charter, his Wroxham-based enterprise, is an unforgettable experience not to be missed. Peter has helped with this section, as has Bob Malster, undoubtedly the greatest living authority on trading wherries.

For the next chapter the inspiration was the family albums of the Boardman family, a treasure trove of Broadland history. Mrs Florence Boardman, wife of the owner and architect of How Hill, started the albums at the turn of the century. She carefully mounted her photographs and labelled many of them in Indian ink. The history of the family and through it the social history of the century emerges with great clarity. I am indebted to the late Humphrey Boardman and his daughter Shirley Place for unrestricted access to this valuable archive.

The third chapter takes us into Suffolk, a wonderfully diverse county which never fails to intrigue and entrance. The Waveney is the link for Suffolk Broadland: the two pleasant market towns of Beccles and Bungay, both set on terraces overlooking the valley, have been influenced over the centuries by their water-borne trade on this river. The Broads become suburban at Oulton Broad: once wild country, later dominated by huge maltings, still later threatened by building development, but even now full of interest and enlivened by regattas and races. Parts of the Suffolk Broadland, including St Olaves, Fritton and Burgh Castle, have been annexed rather ungraciously by Norfolk as a result of 1974 boundary changes.

The familiar *Wind in the Willows* quotation which is used as a title for the next chapter might be regarded by some as unfair: though the average Broadsman is always messing about in, with, or around boats, he takes it very seriously. The boat building and hiring industries are a dominant feature of the life and economy of the Broads. There are many ways to enjoy the Broads but only one way to understand them. It is essential to get out on to the water, in all weathers and in all seasons, before the real essence of the Broads comes into focus. They provide a shallow, safe and lock-free navigation which has given an introduction to boating for millions: the English see themselves as a nautical race and the Broads environment gives them a chance to prove it. The Broads holiday experience has however changed over the years. In the early days the large cabin yachts provided space and comfort: the work of sailing and catering was undertaken by a paid crew. Later, the Broads experience became available to a wider range of people and many of the boats were equipped for a kind of aquatic camping experience. Holiday-makers could imagine themselves as adventuring pioneers, tying up overnight in the reeds, putting up an awning across the well of their hired yacht, and sleeping in narrow berths on the floor. Now, of course, holiday-makers expect comfort, space, luxury – and television.

Chapter five is all about people. Sometimes, looking through an old album, or a battered Oxo tin of old photographs, nostalgia gives way to a feeling of deep sadness. It is all too easy to linger over a tattered photograph of children and dwell on their faces thinking how their whole lives have been and gone and how they and their families have suffered in two world wars, depressions, floods and other misfortunes, and of pleasures and excitements which have passed by. Two people who can speak eloquently of the changes in Broadland life over this century have helped with this section. Arthur Lark, brought up on the edge of the Breydon marshes, and Bertie High, raised in the heart of the Halvergate marshes at his father's mill, have lent photographs and given an insight into this lost world.

The penultimate chapter takes its title from a line in Milton's *Paradise Lost*, perhaps appropriately since most Broadland villages have changed drastically as the motor car has come to dominate. A more tranquil rural past is conjured up by these pictures although they only tell part of the story: the harsh reality of village life should not be forgotten. The last chapter is unashamedly a selection of pictures that I wanted to include but couldn't logically put anywhere else. The 'And Finally' heading borrowed from ITN's *News at Ten* enables inclusion of some aspects of the Broads which might otherwise have been forgotten.

Looking back to the past in a variety of ways, is a source of pleasure and interest to almost everyone. The past has a real and continuing significance for us all; our own past, our family history, the story of our own area, county or nation – such things determine what we think, what we do, even define our identity. As Graham Swift put it in *Waterland*: 'Life is one tenth Here and Now, nine-tenths a history lesson'. The present evaporates into the past with every passing second, and the future is invariably alarming and unsettling, almost always out of our control. The past is ours to keep, it is constant and unchanging; it guides our actions and steers us through our everyday lives. Perhaps that is why so many people enjoy looking at old photographs, a tangible link with the shared experience which is our recent history.

CHAPTER ONE

THE NORFOLK WHERRY

A trading wherry lowers its sail on the approach to Ludham Bridge and a pleasure wherry is moored by the mill, c. 1920.

Creeds are denied, the nations disagree,
Men ask, what use? and nobody replies;
But here, where the grey broad meets the grey skies,
The creaking wherry, leaning her brown sail,
Steals on, along the fen,
She bears, within her, barrel, box and bale,
A day's quietus to the wants of men;
Happy the men who man her, happy she.

John Masefield, 'The Norfolk Wherry', 1937.

The wherry *Spray* tied up in the Port of Norwich, January 1933. Her skipper, William Royall, who was eighty when this picture was taken, is coming alongside in a punt. The *Spray* was the last wherry without the characteristic white snout.

Spectators making good use of a trading wherry at Potter Heigham Regatta, *c.* 1928. The more distant wherry is in use as the Regatta Committee Boat, and the boat sheds are in the process of being re-thatched.

A trading wherry at Ellingham Mill, *c.* 1925. The skipper and his mate are about to raise the sail, having just negotiated one of the locks on this part of the River Waveney. Ellingham Mill has a long and eventful history: in 1908 the miller George Butler was found hanging, his suicide brought on by business worries.

A trading wherry makes good use of a south-westerly wind as it heads towards Lowestoft along Oulton Dyke, *c.* 1912.

The trading wherry *Zulu* on the River Waveney near Bungay, *c*. 1905. The day is nearly dead calm and the skipper has fitted a bonnet to his sail (a yard of extra sail attached to the base of the mainsail) to catch every breath of wind. Note the profusion of waterweed in the river.

Loddon Red Cross Hospital outing, 6 August 1917. An iron trading wherry doubles as a 'troopship', taking soldiers and sailors recovering from war wounds on a much needed pleasure cruise on the River Chet.

The famous trading wherry *Albion* noses her way into Bungay Staithe, 1917. The *Albion*, 100 years old in 1998, has a smooth carvel-built hull, unlike the more typical clinker build. Note that the approach to the staithe had become overgrown during the war years.

Trading wherries at the Wherry Hotel, Oulton Broad, *c.* 1912. On the left, the *Meteor* from Surlingham is just getting under way: the other vessel may well be awaiting a chance to slip through Mutford Lock to the Port of Lowestoft.

The trading wherry *Gertrude* in the Port of Norwich, *c.* 1934. Her gaff and sail are swung round completely to avoid the hold while unloading. Also in view is the steam launch *Alda*.

The trading wherry *Hilda*, March 1940. The *Hilda* was frozen in at the end of 1939 and the water level dropped, causing the ice to break up on the outward side. The wherry inevitably canted over and sank. This photograph was taken by Horace Bolingbroke a few months later.

The trading wherry *Dispatch*, 25 April 1940. Another of Horace Bolingbroke's pictures shows the *Dispatch* under motor passing through the New Cut at Thorpe St Andrew. The skipper George Rump is on the right-hand side; his unnamed mate has the tiller.

Acle Bridge, *c.* 1898. A Norwich-based trading wherry is unloading a cargo of what appears to be marl, chalky clay. The beautiful medieval bridge was replaced in 1932 and this in turn was renewed in 1997.

The trading wherry *Dispatch*, September 1932.
Another calm day brings hard work: even
though the wherry is unladen, much effort
goes into quanting along the River Yare at
Thorpe. Note the white sail, still new.

Wroxham Broad, August 1919. Two pleasure wherries and a trader take their places for a light-hearted
race as part of this first regatta after the First World War – although calm conditions must have made this
a very slow race.

Beccles Quay, *c.* 1905. Two wherries are seen against a backdrop of the waterside building at Beccles. Note the graffiti on the doors and wall of Pells' shed to the left.

Beccles Quay, *c.* 1905. Undoubtedly taken on the same day as the previous photograph, this view reveals that the wherry on the left in that shot is in fact the *Olive* of Lowestoft. *Olive*, a 28-ton vessel, was actually built in Beccles by Wrights.

The *Albion*, 1950. The Norfolk Wherry Trust was established in 1949 and its first task was to return the *Albion* to sailing order. This photograph shows her looking smart – and somewhat overloaded – at the Trust's fête at Brundall on the River Yare.

The pleasure wherry Red Rover, Horning, c. 1930. In the early years of pleasure cruising, trading wherries might be swept out to provide temporary holiday craft, but this was most unsatisfactory, especially for ladies. Some trading wherries like Red Rover were converted into pleasure wherries, but far superior were vessels specially built for pleasure use. Examples included Bramble, Solace, Hathor, Dragon, Rambler and Sunbeam. The most sophisticated wherries were wherry yachts, with the traditional single mast, gaff and square mainsail, but with the smooth hull of a yacht, and a comfortable counter-stern for stylish water-borne picnics.

Wherries at Oulton Broad, 1951. The *Albion* is to the front of the picture and in the background can be seen pleasure wherries *Ardea* (stern on), which still survives in Paris as a houseboat, and *Claudian*.

The pleasure wherry *Bramble* at Oulton Broad, *c.* 1930. It could be hired from Leo Robinson's yard, with two attendants and a sailing dinghy, for £28 5s during the high season.

Trading wherry, Womack Staithe, Ludham, *c.* 1912. Again there is very little wind and the skipper's mate is forced to make use of the quant pole.

The pleasure wherry *Black Prince* at Stalham, 1935. This vessel was hired out in its later years as a 'motor wherry', which was highly convenient for large families. They could sit on top of the cabin without having to make way for sails and other inconveniences! Even so, the Beccles-based hirers still provided a skipper 'for looking after the engine'.

Golden Hind at Wroxham, *c.* 1931. One of the finest of all the wherry yachts, this was the pride of John Loynes' fleet: it boasted a piano, electric light, and a bathroom. It also had a 9 hp Thornycroft engine and a sailing dinghy: as usual it was hired out with two attendants.

John Loynes' yard, Wroxham Bridge, *c.* 1935. A Saturday in summer, showing three wherry yachts about to start their cruises, the *Golden Hind* closest to the camera.

On board the pleasure wherry *Hathor*, 1909. This famous wherry was designed by Edward Thomas Boardman, the How Hill architect, for his sisters in law Ethel and Helen Colman. It was built by Halls of Reedham in 1905. The photograph shows Christopher Boardman (left) and his brothers, twins Humphrey and Stuart (standing).

CHAPTER TWO

LIFE ON THE HILL

The Boardman twins, Humphrey and Stuart, enjoy their pedal cars at How Hill, September 1909.

With all the smell of autumn dew,
The sense of oldness, not new,
The water like glass,
Shimmers through reeds and grass.

Coloured reflections ripple on the broad,
While you hear a faint chirp from a far-off bird.
The feeling I get is the feeling of still,
That's what it's like on the broads at How Hill.

Martin Dring (aged 11), 'The Wood'.

Mrs Florence Boardman with her daughter
Joan Caroline, June 1902. Edward Thomas
Boardman married Florence Esther Colman in
1898 and they lived in Town Close House,
Norwich. However, they purchased the Mill
House at How Hill, Ludham, in 1902 and then
started to plan their holiday home at How Hill,
completed in 1905. Joan was born on
14 January 1902.

Nanny Mary Rolfe with Joan Boardman at How Hill Staithe, 1903. By the time this photograph was taken,
Joan was eighteen months old.

Nanny Rolfe with Joan, Nanny Cork with Christopher Boardman, 1904. Christopher Alan was born on 11 June 1903. Nurse Florence Cork, known as Corkie since she shared her first name with Mrs Boardman, was at the beginning of her life's work in service with the Boardman family.

Christopher Boardman on the cabin roof of the pleasure wherry *Hathor*, 8 August 1911. The Colman and Boardman families had many blissful summer cruises on the *Hathor*. This photograph was taken during the Womack Regatta.

Beside the River Ant at How Hill, 30 April 1912. One of the Boardman twins watches as his brother Christopher gets close to nature. This delightful scene uncannily presages the modern-day role of How Hill as an aquatic ecology study centre for children.

Joan meets an obstacle, How Hill, 30 April 1912. The steam engine must have seemed like something from another world but Joan's well-schooled pony took it in her stride.

The front lawn at How Hill, August 1925. Bob Platford is seen mowing the lawn: the flower beds have since been reduced to give room for paving outside the front of the house.

The Ludham to Horning road, August 1912. Edward Thomas Boardman is seen inspecting the depth of this spectacular summer flood on the west side of Ludham Bridge.

How Hill Farm, 1932. At the end of a grand summer, the corn stacks are carefully put together – a classic rural scene we shall never see again.

Three of the farm workers on top of a corn stack, How Hill Farm, 1932. Note the fields beyond, thick with corn stooks: sheaves in groups of ten or twelve standing to dry in the sun.

How Hill Farm, 1928. Humphrey Boardman's future wife Vera adds a touch of glamour to this harvest scene.

A shooting party, How Hill, Christmas 1929. Members of the Boardman family and their guests together with some of the estate workers take a lunch break outside Crome's Farmhouse.

Humphrey Boardman, April 1927. This photograph was taken on Crome's Broad, part of the How Hill estate, and records an unusually close encounter with a coot.

How Hill, January 1931. The picture shows Humphrey Boardman's new 12 hp Austin, with its hood in place.

The Mill House, How Hill, 12 October 1929.
Very best clothes for estate worker Bob Platford
as he prepares to give his niece away on her
wedding day.

How Hill, 1931. Edward Thomas Boardman (right) gives orders for snow clearance to his garden worker
Mr Nudd, with pickaxe, and his farm manager Mr Bloom.

In the lane outside How Hill, August 1929. Edward Thomas Boardman (right) is seen discussing the day's work with his farm foreman Mr Bloom. The How Hill farm had been tenanted until Michaelmas 1926 but Mr Boardman and his son Stuart took it in hand: fruit farming and fattening bullocks were two of the farm's main concerns. There were ten full-time workers in addition to the foreman; Stuart's son Peter still farms here with only one farm worker.

The Mill, How Hill, 1921. Edward Boardman's first purchase in 1902 of land at How Hill included the Mill House and an old corn windmill. The ground floor of the mill was converted into a garage and workshop. This picture shows the Boardman brothers and friends: Christopher (extreme right) is on the pillion seat of a Zenith motorcycle, but his young brother Michael is on a toy scooter; Humphrey is on the back of the left-hand bike, Stuart on the middle machine.

Mr Nudd, How Hill, 1922. Edward Boardman's gardens were his lifelong joy and passion, and he was most meticulous about all aspects of the work in them. Mr Nudd was for many years under-gardener on the How Hill estate.

Outside the Mill House, How Hill, 1921. These ladies were friends of the Boardman family, but for once Mrs Boardman did not record details: usually her neat Indian ink script is to be found close to each photograph. This picture is included because of the car: a rare Carden four wheeler. Perhaps it was slow to start: Joan is at the rear giving a gentle push.

How Hill Staithe, 1931. Michael Boardman is given a lesson in sculling by his elder brother Humphrey, on the bank. Humphrey, an international oarsman, coached Cambridge University boat crews so Michael had the best possible tuition.

Thatching outbuildings at the rear of How Hill, June 1926. The outbuildings are now joined to the house, and the loft which is in the process of being thatched is now my office. The thatch has lasted well and will have to last many more years yet. Note the gutters: thatched houses usually do not have them as they fill with debris at every storm.

CHAPTER THREE

INTO SUFFOLK

Evening at Oulton Broad.

When pool and stream were frozen hard,
And cattle stayed within the yard;
When elms were red, and ash-trees black,
And sparrows robbed the farmer's stack;
When tilth and fallow changed to stone,
And hoodies fought around a bone;
When hands were numb and minds depressed,
When snow the naked trees had dressed;
Said I, I will away from here
In this hard season of the year.

Yet here I stay and years go by,
And Suffolk knows the reason why.

Charles H. Lay, 'To Suffolk', 1928.

The tower mill, Bungay, *c.* 1910. This fine corn mill was built in 1830 and was last worked in 1918; the last miller was William Parker. The building was later converted into a house, but it has long since lost both cap and sails.

Bungay, August 1912. The August flood of 1912 was one of the most catastrophic in East Anglia's history. This shows the floor of the Waveney valley from the Earsham dam. The road from Norfolk is marked by the railings. The town itself is well placed to avoid floods, and the castle and church occupy the higher ground.

The staithe, Bungay, 1925. The Waveney navigation, upstream of Beccles Bridge, depended upon three locks: Shipmeadow (or Geldeston), Ellingham and Wainford. Since the distance by road between Beccles and Bungay is only a matter of 5 miles, the Bungay Staithe became much less regularly used after the First World War. Three locks and a shallow, weedy, meandering river ensured that most wherrymen went no further upriver than Beccles. The navigation, once the source of Bungay's prosperity, finally closed in 1934.

Gillingham dam from Beccles Bridge, August 1912. This flood scene is taken looking along the main road towards Gillingham and Norwich.

Gillingham dam, Beccles, August 1912. The message on the back of this postcard view reads: 'Just got this card of the Dam. Boats were rowed right up to Mrs Lane's house. Trees were uprooted'. The children seem to have enjoyed it, though.

Bridge Street, Beccles, 1912. The main part of Beccles, like Bungay, is higher and therefore safe from flooding. But Bridge Street inevitably suffered from the surge of water following the 6 in of rain which fell in 12 hours on 26 August 1912.

View from Beccles Bridge, 28 August 1912. Two days after the storm and the scene is still one of surging river water and floods on all sides. This is another postcard view and it was sent on 8 September – the sender noted 'water has gone down a lot but there is still plenty left'.

Beccles Regatta, August 1904. A wonderfully calm day, but not a day for sailing. Both the yachts under way have distinctive rigs but the one on the left is of a class unique to the Waveney Sailing Club. It is a 16 ft half-decked open boat; the class was defined in 1896 and the most successful of its type was the *Unit*, which won thirty-three out of forty-three races in her first season.

Beccles Regatta, 1936. Racing towards the camera are Brown Boats, more properly called Broads One-Designs, 24 ft overall and 16 ft on the waterline. The class made its debut at Oulton Broad on Whit Monday 1901. The number of the leading boat is hidden but behind her are *Bittern* (No. 12), *Turnstone* (No. 15), *Kingfisher* (No. 7), *Dabchick* (No. 6) and *Peewit* (No. 5).

Beccles Regatta, 1951. Officiating is Mr Barber, who was, in fact, a barber – he ran a shop in Smallgate in Beccles.

Beccles Regatta, 1936. This picture shows White Boats racing on the River Waveney. These are officially Yare and Bure One-Designs, a class which originated in 1908. Nearest the camera is *Water Soldier* and in front of her is *Arrowhead*. Now most of the class are named after butterflies and moths, real or imaginary.

Boaters Hills on the River Waveney, *c.* 1931. This was a popular spot for picnics and days out, close to Beccles and with fine views across the Waveney valley. The motor cruiser *Enchantress*, from Oulton Broad, is seen moored in this picture. More details of this noble craft are given on p. 55.

Fritton Lake, *c.* 1912. The three-mile lake at Fritton is not accessible from the river and it remains a popular haunt for fishermen and day trippers to this day. Rowing boats were available for hire from Old Hall Staithe and teas were provided.

Fritton Decoy, *c.* 1900. Fritton's greatest claim to fame is undoubtedly its duck decoy. By means of some tame ducks and with the aid of a trained dog, wild ducks were decoyed from the main lake up into the ever narrowing channels which led to a funnel-shaped enclosure. The decoyman could then kill the ducks by a skilful flick of the wrist – the birds were therefore undamaged, unlike those which had been shot. Over the period of fifteen years to 1877, some 13,421 birds were trapped at Fritton Decoy.

The *Elizabeth Simpson*, Gorleston Harbour, *c.* 1925. *Elizabeth Simpson* was a famous private or volunteer lifeboat which was on call at Gorleston for fifty years, 1889 to 1939. She stayed in her boathouse throughout the Second World War and was then refitted as a passenger launch at Herbert Woods' yard in Potter Heigham.

Elizabeth Simpson, Oulton Broad, *c.* 1958. When she was no longer in use as a lifeboat, her new owner William Beale ran trips at Oulton Broad and Lowestoft. She eventually returned to Gorleston for harbour trips in 1969.

Oulton Broad, 1905. The picture shows one of the many cruiser races held at Oulton in summer. Cruising yachts had fixed cabin tops, so were comfortable, but their huge sails and long bowsprits made them exciting to handle. Notable vessels of the time included *White Wings*, *Castanet* and *Sayonara*.

Another view of the same cruiser race, Oulton Broad, 1905. Oulton Broad has always been one of the largest yachting centres in Broadland; in 1895 a sailing club was established there, the Waveney Sailing Club. This was open to all – amateur, professional, gentlemen or working men, which at the time was most unusual – and it had over 200 members by 1902.

Leo Robinson's yard, Oulton Broad, *c.* 1914. Something of a mystery, this view appears to show a Broads cruiser modified for war service. The picture belongs to Stuart Press: any information would be welcome.

Leo Robinson's yard, Oulton Broad, *c.* 1937. Astonishingly, this is the same location as the preceding picture. Several splendid cruisers await their hirers, and one is being repainted – in the water. On the extreme left, stern on, is the *Waveney*, built in 1928.

Oulton Broad, August 1912. The 1912 floods were not just a cloudburst – they were accompanied by a fearful gale. The aftermath of such a storm – in August, the high season – is clear in this view: two large sailing cruisers are awash.

Oulton Broad, *c.* 1900. Oulton has always been the most suburban of all the Broads, with maltings, houses and inns on its shore. But before it became devoted to pleasure boating, there were some who found other sport there. This picture shows one of the last of the Oulton wildfowlers on the roof of his houseboat.

Viscountess Bury, Oulton Broad, *c.* 1900. Some fine costumes are given an airing on a day trip on the Broads, on board the *Viscountess Bury*. In the foreground is the top (or hood) of a trading wherry.

Mutford Lock, Oulton Broad, *c.* 1919. The lock connects the Broads to Lake Lothing and Lowestoft Harbour and thence the sea. Wisely, few holidaymakers make the connection and of course hire-craft are not allowed through. The lock has recently been renovated but the area is now dominated by a very busy main road.

Brown Boats, Oulton Broad, 1913. The picture reveals light airs giving the Broads One-Design skippers a frustrating race, but not without incident. The rigging of *Teal* (No. 2) has actually fouled the boom of *Snipe* (No. 10).

Brown Boats, Oulton Broad, 1913. The same fleet of Broads One-Designs are this time enjoying breezier conditions. *Teal* (No. 2) and *Peewit* (No. 5) are neck and neck, closely followed by *Mallard* (No. 14) and *Dotterel* (No. 8). On the left of the picture are *Dabchick* (No. 6), *Dunlin* (No. 1) and *Flittermouse* (No. 3).

Regatta at Oulton Broad, 1938. This picture is taken on another good sailing day: four of the craft shown are White Boats, Yare and Bure One-Designs. Nearest the camera is *Alalanta* (No. 17).

Nicholas Everitt Park, Oulton Broad, 1925. The park commemorates one of the most notable names of Broads history, Nicholas Everitt, a lawyer and Broadland author. The 15½ acres of land, with 590 yd of frontage on the Broad, was presented to Lowestoft Corporation by Mr Howard Hollingworth who had bought it after Everitt's death.

Oulton Broad, 1953. The disastrous east coast floods of 31 January 1953 caused widespread damage in Broadland. This shows the quayside and park in early February; a 16 ft breach in the bank between Lake Lothing and the Broad brought a torrent of flood water through the shops on Bridge Road, which itself was undermined by the surge.

Drainage mill, River Waveney, 1912. Most of the windmills which remain in the Broads have fantails to turn them into the wind and patent sails like a series of louvres which can be adjusted by means of a single endless chain. However, before 1807 the typical mill was like the one in this picture, turned to wind manually by means of tailpoles and with lattice sails which were draped laboriously with sailcloth. This mill at Oulton Marsh was one of the last survivors of the older type.

W.B. Hoseason, Oulton Broad, 1938. William Ballantyne or 'Wally' Hoseason, a Shetlander, became Harbour Master at Oulton Broad for Lowestoft Corporation in the early 1930s. His first venture into hiring boats was in the summer of 1944 when he let moored cruisers as holiday houseboats for families evacuated from London to East Anglia. The craft could not be moved, as petrol was rationed and the Broads had too many obstacles – half-wrecked vessels positioned to prevent enemy seaplane landings. Hoseason's first brochure was a mere four pages (1946).

Hoseason's brochure, 1951. W.B. Hoseason died in 1950 and his son James, then in his early twenties, took over the business. The 1951 brochure lists a selection of cruisers and yachts, houseboats and even caravans: perhaps the oddest let was a converted single-decker bus at Horsey. It was called Annette, was sited on a farm between the dunes and the mere, and terms ranged from £5 to £8 a week.

The *Water Fly* at St Olaves, *c.* 1912. Pleasure steamers operated by The Yarmouth and Gorleston Steamboat Company carried trippers between Norwich, Yarmouth and Lowestoft on the Rivers Yare and Waveney. St Olaves was a popular destination because passengers could then be transported to the gardens at Fritton Lake for an inclusive ticket price.

St Olaves Bridge, *c.* 1948. St Olaves village was in Suffolk at the time, but since 1974 has been officially part of Norfolk. The bridge was completed in October 1847 under the supervision of George Edwards JP, engineer. It is the third bridge at this important crossing, the first being erected in about 1500 and the second in 1768.

CHAPTER FOUR

'SIMPLY MESSING ABOUT IN BOATS'

Parasols on Ranworth Broad, c. 1934.

Listen my friends! One evening at the close
Of dinner, from the cabin we arose,
Gazed o'er old Potter Heigham, where we lay
With yachts and wherries moored in two long rows.

Truly, in every Broad may be espied
Some subtle charm, to blinder eyes denied;
Each river is a mirror that reflects
The changing beauty of its reed-girt side.

'Tolly', 'The Rubaiyát of Potter Heigham', August 1911.

South Walsham, August 1919. This photograph is taken from a small album presented to 'The Skipper' by R. Godfrey Crittall following a family cruise. Unfortunately neither the skipper's name nor that of the yacht is recorded but it is believed to be the *Kingfisher*. This picture shows the family at breakfast.

Wroxham Broad, August 1919. The skipper mentioned above rows across to a pleasure wherry. This is the *Liberty*, built by Ernest collins of Wroxham, and almost unique among Pleasure Wherries in that her hull was carvel built (note the smooth sides).

The Woods End, Bramerton, 1937. A few miles downstream from Norwich on the River Yare this pub was, and is, a popular destination for boating parties. The photograph shows a trading wherry and a steam launch preparing to depart.

Yare Sailing Club houseboat, 1906. This vessel was purpose-built for the club, founded in 1876. Supporters of the club took shares of £1 each to fund the project and then rented the houseboat to the club. The houseboat was built by Ernest Collins of Wroxham and was big enough to provide overnight accommodation and catering for members. The club amalgamated with the Bure Sailing Club in 1907.

Horning Mill, *c.* 1898. This bend of the River Bure is now known as Swan Corner but this photograph pre-dates the building of the Swan public house on the site.

Stokesby Ferry Inn, *c.* 1931. The sloop-rigged yacht tied up at the inn is the *Penelope*, on hire from W.S. Parker at Oulton Broad. Five people could enjoy a week's cruise in this 35 ft boat for a total of £13 in the high season of 1931, dinghy included.

Rambler, Oulton Broad, *c.* 1937. Leo Robinson of Oulton Broad offered this unique craft for hire; she was basically a wherry yacht but with a raked stern and forepeak. The crew, a skipper and a steward, slept in the bow, as usual, and *Rambler* could sleep ten guests in style and comfort.

Enchantress, Oulton Broad, 1929. A superbly equipped 60 ft motor cruiser, fitted throughout in teak, this was a magnificent launch, also on hire from Leo Robinson. Blakes' 1931 catalogue says of her: 'Completely fitted with everything of first-class quality for living and sleeping on board. . . . Crew – two in number – skilled engineer acting as skipper, and steward who attends to all cooking'. She had seven berths and the hire charge was £30 for a week in August, but £19 10s in early and late season.

SS *Jenny Lind*, near Bramerton, *c.* 1908. For a few shillings a river trip from the quay at Foundry Bridge, Norwich to Yarmouth, to Reedham, to Bramerton, to Brundall Gardens, or to Oulton Broad provided a happy excursion.

Eel's Foot Inn, Ormesby St Michael, *c.* 1935. The clear, enclosed waters of Ormesby Broad always provided superb fishing, away from the bustle of motor cruisers and yachts on the main river system. The Eel's Foot was an ideal place for trippers from Yarmouth to hire a fishing boat for the day.

Martham, River Thurne, c. 1936. The Broads have always enjoyed a reputation for easy sailing but the combination of a narrow river and yachts too close together seems to have resulted in navigational chaos on this occasion.

Hickling Broad, c. 1928. Emma Turner, a noted photographer and expert ornithologist, spent a good deal of time in and around her houseboat on Hickling Broad. This picture shows Miss Turner at her houseboat where she did much of the work for her classic book Broadland Birds.

Potter Heigham Regatta, 1931. The barrel race, shown here, must have been a highly entertaining event: certainly it drew a large crowd. Also in the photograph are the motor cruiser *Orellana* and the wherry yacht *Olive*.

Potter Heigham Regatta, 1931. Another unpredictable event which appears to involve crossing the river on a raft and repelling boarders. The motor cruiser is a Herbert Woods boat, one of the Speed of Light class.

Potter Heigham, *c.* 1938. The yacht is one of the Leading Lady class, Herbert Woods' classic Broads sailing cruisers. As the Blakes 1938 catalogue puts it, 'these handsome craft represent the latest and most modern development of sailing yachts ever offered for hire on the Broads'. Built of mahogany, these 32 ft yachts were fast and full of innovations and were offered for £12 10s per week in the high season.

Potter Heigham, *c.* 1908. This is another regatta scene but an earlier event with pretty little lug-sail dinghies competing on the River Thurne, seen from the medieval bridge.

Potter Heigham, *c.* 1930. Another view from the old bridge, this time the image shows the yards of both George Applegate Jr and Bob Applegate. The nearest moored craft is *The Hope*, a 39 ft gunter rigged yacht offered with an attendant by George Applegate at £13 15*s* in the high season.

Broads-Haven, Potter Heigham, 1934. Herbert Woods, perhaps the most far-sighted of all the Broads entrepreneurs, established a mooring basin and yard at Potter Heigham on a scale that older yards were soon to envy. He provided garaging for hirers' cars, which inevitably took his business 'up-market'. The cruisers in this shot are all Light class, with names such as *Princess of Light*, *Heiress of Light* and *Peeress of Light*.

The *Madie*, Ranworth, *c.* 1934. A famous Broads racing yacht and still in sailing order today, *Madie* was originally called *Madge* but the change of a single letter gave much greater distinction. Built in 1906 by Ernest Collins of Wroxham, she achieved great early success when raced by Charlie 'Dodger' Green for her owner, Mr T.A. Cook.

Wroxham Bridge, *c.* 1895. This famous picture shows *The Swan*, a 4-ton yacht built for G. Christopher Davies by Gibbs and Reynolds at Coldham Hall in 1876. Davies is regarded as the author who did most to promote the Broads: he is undoubtedly in this photograph – perhaps he is the bow-tied pipe-smoking gentleman standing on the counter stern.

Wroxham Broad, 1938. A race for Norfolk One-Designs is under way. These 14 ft mahogany dinghies were first built by Herbert Woods at Potter Heigham as a much cheaper alternative to the International 14 class. Successful local helmsmen such as Ian Macintosh, Martin Broom and Raymond Jeckells proved their ability in these dinghies soon after the war.

The Norfolk Broads Yacht Club, Wroxham Broad, c. 1959. The club was formed in October 1937 when the opportunity arose to lease Wroxham Broad; four clubs came together to seize this chance. The picture shows the open fronted 'Tea Pavilion' which was officially opened in Wroxham Week, 1939.

Melisande, Wroxham, Whitsun 1935. The picture shows Graham Bunn at the controls of this superb launch. As proprietor of Windboats, Mr Bunn achieved a reputation as an eccentric and as a minor poet, but also as a perfectionist: his craft, whether for hire or sale, were very well equipped and highly finished and invariably had powerful engines.

River Bure, Wroxham, July 1929. This view looking upstream towards the railway shows the usual variety of craft. In the foreground is *Katrina*, a three-cabin cruiser fitted throughout in teak.

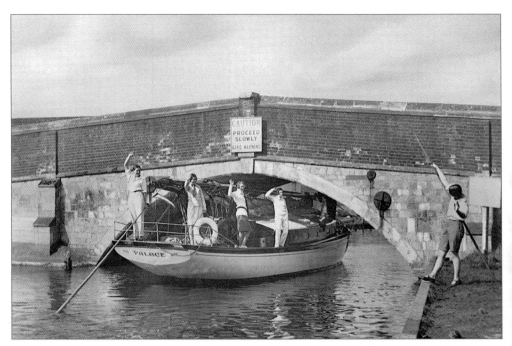

Wroxham Bridge, *c.* 1937. The yacht *Palace* slips quietly under the bridge: one of the smartest of Broads craft, she was 47 ft long, fully fitted inside in mahogany, with electric light and cabin space for seven berths (and an extra mattress if required to make room for an eighth guest). With attendant, the hire charges ranged from £11 per week low season to £16 10s in August 1937.

E. & C. Press's yard, Wroxham, *c.* 1934. The yacht is *Zephyr*, sloop rigged and built of bright varnished mahogany. Behind her is the cruiser *Grey Dawn*, at that time one of the finest motor cruisers on the Broads and later rented out as a houseboat within view of Daisy Broad.

Saturday morning, Loynes' yard, Wroxham, *c.* 1935. The frenetic activity of 'changeover day' is captured in this superb view at the height of the holiday season: Jack Powles' and Ernest Collins' yards are in the background.

The River Bure at Horning, *c.* 1934. This holiday snapshot shows one of the three *Ripple* yachts which could be hired from John Loynes' yard at Wroxham. Sloop rigged, 34 ft long, and smart, these were ideal for family holidays afloat.

On board *Ripple*, Horning, *c.* 1934. The pictures on this page and the next two pages were taken from the same holiday album as the preceding shot. They reveal a happy cruise by several groups of friends. The pictures were loaned by Peter Bower of Wherry Yacht Charter at Wroxham.

Sultan, Horning, *c.* 1934. *Sultan*, built in 1928, was a spacious 33 ft 6 in motor cruiser, on hire from H.C. Banham of Horning. On this occasion the friends hiring her took the option of employing an attendant but she still went aground: the attendant then had the task of single-handedly getting her under way.

On board the *Sultan*, Horning, *c.* 1934. *Sultan* only had berths for six, so for this group photograph the friends were joined by those on board *Ripple* and a sister ship of *Sultan*, probably the *Ranee*.

On board the *Sultan*, *c.* 1934. There never seemed much doubt, until quite recently, as to the division of labour on board. Men very quickly bought themselves skippers' caps at Roys of Wroxham and the ladies had to undertake the catering: on this occasion peeling the potatoes.

South Walsham, *c.* 1934. This is another shot
from the holiday album, included simply
because it is a delightful reminder of carefree
summer days.

Provisioning, Ranworth, *c.* 1934. It was easy to obtain supplies of fresh food from most villages and of
course Roys of Wroxham could provide you with enough for an entire cruise. Nonetheless there was an
opportunity for trading on the water, and the novelty of buying fresh supplies from a boatman was often
too great to resist.

Thurne Dyke, *c.* 1928. This rather austere photograph is included to show how open the Broads landscape used to be, and also for the view of the farmhouse, now completely vanished. The moored yacht on the left is called *Freedom*, a simple 22 ft sloop suitable for four people, as long as two of them slept on mattresses placed on the cabin floor.

Ranworth, Maltsters' Staithe, *c.* 1937. Tied up at the quayside are two Light class boats from Herbert Woods of Potter Heigham and *Ailsa Craig II* from Chumley & Hawke Ltd of Horning.

Thorpe village, River Yare, *c.* 1936. Thorpe was often described as the Richmond of Norfolk: a wooded, hilly suburb by the river. Jenner's boat yard can be seen and on the river is one of this firm's typical small family hire cruisers.

Windboats at Wroxham, 1935. Graham Bunn's fleet of hire cruisers were most impressive. *Eddy Wind One* (on the left) was described as 'four fathoms of permanent varnished teak with a complete home inside . . . a mighty atom, controllable by the novice'. The larger craft shown is *Fair Wind One*: 'highly original and stylish appearance, extreme comfort, and perfect response to all wishes of the hirer and his party . . . a complete and well-tested craft in which you can take your holiday with perfect assurance'.

Delight XI on the River Thurne, *c.* 1936. The fleet of Delight class motor cruisers from Herbert Woods'
Potter Heigham yard were ideal for two or three adults. The boats were numbered – there were twelve in
all – and the odd numbers had a different internal arrangement from the even numbers.

Shimmer of Light, Potter Heigham, *c.* 1935. This was another one of Herbert Woods' modern fleet of
motor cruisers which did so much to bring convenience and style to Broads holidays of this period. There
were berths for five people on board, 'giving extreme privacy in their excellent arrangement': there was
also a 5 ft bath and two WCs. Terms per week ranged from £11 to £16 in 1937 but by 1950 this had risen
to between £28 and £35.

Sable, *Sirocco* and *Sonata*, Wroxham, 1930. These motor cruisers were part of the hire fleet of George Smith and Sons of Wroxham. *Sable*, 30 ft long, was built in 1926; the other two boats were 32 ft long and were built in the following two years. They were 'extremely commodious and modern', and were finished inside in teak and mahogany: all the deck fittings were nickel plated.

Houseboat at Horning, *c.* 1958. Houseboats are very nearly a thing of the past, as modern planners do not approve, but they were once very popular throughout the district. This picture shows *Glen Mist*, belonging to A.H. Carr at Horning – £24 per week in high season 1958.

Kathleen at Beccles, July 1904. This picture shows an all-male and rather sombre cruise on the River Waveney on board a stately steam launch: note the skipper towards the rear. There was an attempt at light-heartedness for the camera in the form of the life belt around the neck of one of the passengers.

Blanche at Coltishall, 1907. This shows a rather happier jaunt on board a steam launch, with lots of well-dressed ladies aboard. *Blanche* took parties on trips from John Loynes' yard at Wroxham Bridge, an elegant diversion.

River Waveney at Burgh St Peter, *c.* 1920. The yacht is the *America*, a 43 ft cutter from Ernest Collins of Wroxham. In the background is the uniquely distinctive tower of St Peter's Church.

Dinghy racing, Burgh St Peter, 4 July 1954. A race for all-comers, with two Norfolk dinghies (B49, B39) and an International 14 (K 512). The message on the back of this photograph reads, cryptically, 'Isis over the line, has to come back', so clearly the start of the race was untidy.

On the Waveney, *c.* 1912. No information is available on this scene, but the accompanying message speaks volumes: 'This is of our boat . . . had a very hot day but wind against us all the time . . . tacking is very boring'.

Adventuress, Oulton Broad, *c.* 1936. One of the smaller yachts in Leo Robinson's hire fleet, the *Adventuress* was 24 ft 6 in long and could sleep four. It was 'specially designed for gentlemen sailing themselves'. Terms ranged from 5 guineas to £8 per week in 1937.

Goldfinch, Oulton Broad, *c.* 1958. The more modern lines of this yacht show that she was built after the Second World War, but already the sailing holiday, so typical of the Broads, was in decline in favour of the easier option of a powered cruise.

Romany, Oulton Broad, *c.* 1946. Built by Leo Robinson in 1930, this was a luxurious 30 ft cruiser, generously appointed and capable of 9 mph. In August 1931 the weekly rate was £14 10s; in August 1952 this had risen to £38 10s.

Spray, Oulton Broad, *c.* 1938. Another vessel from the hire fleet of Leo Robinson, the *Spray* was suitable for a party of three people although only 21 ft long. Most yards were constantly improving not only their fleet but the boats themselves: earlier photographs show the three upper portholes as tiny circles.

Humphrey Boardman sculling on the Bure, Horning, 1927. Humphrey was an accomplished oarsman, representing Trinity College, Cambridge University and Great Britain in both the 1928 Olympic Games and the 1930 Commonwealth Games. In those days the Commonwealth Games were much grander than the Olympics and Humphrey won two gold medals at Hamilton, Canada, in the 1930 event.

Seagull, at Horning, *c.* 1935. A motor cruiser from Harts of Thorpe which could sleep eight people, *Seagull* was 35 ft long. Two points in the 1931 Blakes' catalogue are noteworthy: 'a wireless receiving set is installed and may be used at a charge of 30s per week', and an attendant came with the boat 'who is engineer and navigator only and does not attend to cooking'.

The *Queen of the Broads*, Horning, *c.* 1937. This steamboat is probably the most famous of all the passenger craft to ply the rivers. Her home mooring was opposite John Loynes' yard downstream of Wroxham Bridge: a perfect location to ensure full cruises, as on this occasion.

A Hustler yacht from Hunter's yard, Ludham, May 1958.

Cyril Hunter who followed his father Percy into the business.

Cyril and Muriel Hunter (on the right) and friends on the *Luna*, on the Bure, *c.* 1937. The boats from Hunter's yard, always well built in mahogany, eventually passed to Norfolk County Council, and are now owned by the Norfolk Heritage Fleet Trust.

Percy Hunter at Womack, *c.* 1950. A traditionalist and a craftsman, Percy Hunter had his own way, and his own pace, of doing things. Uniquely, his fleet still sails – and who could ask for a finer legacy?

C H A P T E R   F I V E

SILENT FACES

A boating party ashore for a picnic at Horsey Staithe, c. 1947.

My homeland! Land of water bird and wherry,
Fierce-bitten fishermen, Viking ancestry!
My heart is lead within me and my spirit
Cries out for your good soil and open sky.

Just let me stay again in that grand county,
Just let me see again the Broadland mists,
Just let me hear those honest Norfolk voices —
Then I can die, and know that heaven exists.

Jeffrey Sorenson, 'Lines By An Exile', 1954.

Bernard Press, Wroxham, *c.* 1961. Mr Press is seen putting the finishing touches to the whale insignia which was adopted by the new Lowestoft-based agency of Bradbeers, a rival for a time of Blakes and Hoseasons. The cruiser is *Press On* from the fleet of C. and G. Press which had recently become part of Brinkcraft Ltd.

Betty 5, Wroxham, *c.* 1961. *Betty 5* was built by Bernard Press and he is seen in this carefully staged publicity photo (note the winter trees) handing over a Kelloggs box to the 'hirer' while Brinkcraft's Swiss owner Fred Brinkoff looks on.

Woodbastwick, 1909. A well-dressed family poses at the cottage gate but no details have been preserved with this charming study.

Woodbastwick, 1909. This is another study from the same private family album as the previous picture. Again no details are available, but it is included because of the delightful costumes and the rather severe faces. The picture is by A. Harl of Norwich.

Jim Vincent with a young marsh harrier, Hickling, *c.* 1930. The marsh harrier is now a characteristic sight over the Broadland reed beds, but between 1870 and 1926 it had become very scarce. Between 1927 and 1947 up to four pairs nested in the Hickling/Horsey area each spring. However, the Montagu's harrier, which is now only a scarce passage migrant in the Broads, bred regularly in the area between 1921 and 1954. The marsh-nesting race of Montagu's harriers is now apparently extinct as this habitat has been abandoned by the species both in the Broads and in Holland.

Marsh harrier nestlings, *c.* 1930. The largest bird of prey to breed in Broadland, the marsh harrier is now a familiar sight. Note the difference in size of these young birds; unless food was abundant it is unlikely that all the young survived.

John Loynes at Wroxham, *c.* 1900. John Loynes is regarded as the first man to hire out holiday craft on the Broads, initially from Elm Hill in Norwich, although in the early 1880s he moved his business to Wroxham. As well as building up a fleet of wherry yachts and 4-ton cutters for hire from his yard next to Wroxham Bridge, Loynes pioneered yacht hire from Stavoren in Holland for English tourists. This came to an end with the anti-Dutch feelings engendered by the Boer War (1899), although Loynes himself still sailed the Dutch waterways until he was well over eighty. He died shortly before the Second World War at the age of ninety-six.

Wherry skipper and lady tourists, August 1919. This charming picture by R. Godfrey Crittall records his family's summer cruise.

Beccles Town football club, 1920/21 season. Most towns and villages had their own amateur teams and the rivalry between them was, then as now, intense. Beccles Town played their home games on a pitch behind the railway station, off The Avenue.

South Walsham School, 1919. This photograph, so typical of class photographs of the period, shows Class 2 of this large village school. The school was built in 1865, extended in 1873, and then enlarged again in 1891 to provide places for 112 children. In 1919 the headmistress was Miss Lilian Amos.

Ludham Home Guard, 1943. This photograph was kindly loaned by Mike Fuller who has succeeded in identifying all but six of the men shown. In the front row the four men on one knee with rifles are, left to right, Stanley Grapes, Eddie Newton, Alfred Gedge and Albert Clarke. In the second row, seated with peaked cap, is Albert Knights; next to him, be-ribboned and spectacled, is Colonel Taylor. Considering that many villagers were away in the regular forces at the time it seems astonishing that Ludham could muster such a large platoon and yet this was only one of many in the area.

Ludham football club, 1946/47 season. In that season the club won three cups, and this picture shows the first team with two of them. The three club officials are, left to right, the President Mr Alcock, Secretary Mr Wright, and (jacket buttoned) Chairman Mr Bird, Ludham schoolmaster.

Filby cricket team, at home, *c.* 1938. Back row, left to right: Alf Nichols, Billy Trett, Derek Dixon, ?, ?, Billy Hudson, Frank Tennant, ?. Front row: Bob Leath, John Trett, Reggie Balls and Gordon Ward.

Filby Brass Band, 1939. Back row, left to right, Jack Kippen, Bertie Hudson, Dick Howlett, Billy Kippen, David Hudson. Middle row: Alan Hudson, Herbert Kippen, Joe Hudson, Charles Fuller, Victor Ward, Arthur Howlett. The youngsters sitting on the ground are Albert Hudson and Leslie Fuller.

Raspberry pickers taking a tea break, Filby, 1950. The raspberry crop, much of it used by the Martham jam factory, was a crucial part of Filby life in the Second World War and the early post-war years. These ladies are in Sidney Hunt's market garden; standing, left to right: Daisy May Kippen, E. Church, Mrs Hudson, Mrs Ruth Hunt, Rose Nichols and Rosie Secker. Seated are Ann and Beryl Smith.

Billy Gaze, Filby, 1920. Billy was from the smithy so perhaps his father made him this tricycle. The blacksmith's premises in Caister Road are now occupied by a petrol filling station.

Cottage gate at the Old Forge, Filby, c. 1914. Left to right, outside their home, are Fred, Margaret, Mabel and Ruth Nichols.

Binder/reaper at Filby, early 1930s. The names of these three horses, worked by Billy Kippen on Chapman's farm in the Pound Lane/Green Lane area of Filby, have been recorded. They are, left to right, Major, Gypsy and Stormer.

The smithy, Caister Road, Filby, *c.* 1910. These harvesters were gathered at the wheelwright's/blacksmith's after the smith had set their scythes ready to mow. No single picture speaks more tellingly of the changes in farming this century.

Ormesby Lane, Filby, 1947. The harshness of the 1947 winter is legendary: all the Broads were frozen for weeks and the fields were several feet deep in snow. By the third week of February large ice floes appeared off the Norfolk coast. Villagers, used to wartime privations and still dogged by rationing and shortages, pulled together to ensure that life could continue. The four Filby men closest to the camera are, left to right, 'Picker' Minister, Joe Brown, Victor Hudson and Bertie Hudson.

Old time dancing, Hickling, c. 1951. As the ration books were finally discarded and life began to get back to normal, villagers decided it was high time to return to the simple pleasures which the war and the years of austerity had pushed aside.

Arthur Lark on the banks of the River Bure, May
1933. Mr Lark, who kindly loaned this
photograph, spent most of his life in and around
the marshes near Breydon Water and Yarmouth.
Here he is seen barrowing clay to repair the
south bank of the River Bure a few miles
upstream of Yarmouth.

Harry Smith, May 1933. The clay had to be shaped to produce a smooth, regular flood bank, strong
enough to withstand the regular tidal surges to which the lower reaches of Broadland rivers are subject.
Harry Smith and Arthur Lark worked together to produce a perfectly symmetrical bank profile, seen
taking shape in this picture.

At High's Mill, Halvergate, 1937. The picture shows Elsie Cannon, future wife of Bertie High, painting a tumbril. She was on holiday from Yarmouth at the time, staying at this remote mill cottage with the High family.

Bertie High, Fleggburgh, 1935. Bertie succeeded his father as marshman at High's Mill in Halvergate, one of six which drained into the Fleet, which in turn emptied into Breydon Water. All six mills were scrapped in 1947 when an electric pump was installed at the end of the Halvergate Fleet. In this picture Mr High is seen working on the fantail of a drainage mill which is now St Margaret's Restaurant, near Acle Bridge.

Bertie High, Halvergate, July 1937. Bertie was the eighth child of James High and was born in 1918. Part of the summer routine was the annual harvest of marsh hay, invaluable fodder for the cattle.

James Thomas High, Halvergate, *c.* 1940. A remote life in the marshes, working for all the local landowners, ditching, draining, embanking, taking cattle to market, mowing hay, weeding out thistles – all this and more was the daily routine of Mr High. He was born in 1871 and worked as a marshman for forty-three years from 1900. He died in 1953.

Reginald March, Stalham, *c.* 1912. Mr March's
father was a basket maker with his own osier
bed, but Reginald went to work in Bristow's
Stalham Mill. Later he went on to manage the
High Street Bakery.

Stalham Moor, 1904. A picnic party, probably the Bristow family with friends, enjoying a summer's day
with a neat but modest alfresco meal.

R.P. Spanton from Stalham, 1 January 1915. As the men went off to the First World War trenches, so the boys were recruited for duties which went somewhat beyond the normal range for Scouts. The Spanton brothers helped with guard duties at the Caister Wireless Station.

Spanton brothers, Caister 1914. Boy Scouts they may have been, but they were big strong lads who were keen and ready to undertake war work. This photograph was also taken at Caister Wireless Station although the boys lived with their family at Stalham.

Bristow's lorry, early 1920s. Mr Bristow was a lay preacher at Stalham chapel and so his lorry was naturally used for the annual chapel outing to Eccles beach. The lorry was actually a Ford Model T car with the back of the car removed and a framework built on instead. Reginald March, in the foreground, was the driver.

Scouts' cooking class, Stalham town hall, 1914. Fourth from left is R. Spanton again. His cousin Jeffrey, on the left in a white collar, was killed in action in 1918. Stalham Elementary School Headmaster Mr Harry Divers is seen at the rear of the class.

C H A P T E R   S I X

'AMONG THE PLEASANT VILLAGES'

Market Place, Bungay, c. 1920.

Historic homesteads, ancient manor farms,
Capacious barns – scarred, lichen-coated, browned
With iron mould; and mills whose sails fling round
In challenge to the unresponsive wold.

Low lying dwellings set with stagnant ponds,
Timber ribbed, plastered, quaintly gabled, thatched;
With open hearths round which is ever matched
The smiling welcome of the flowered garths.

Herbert Hudson, 'Suffolk', 1927.

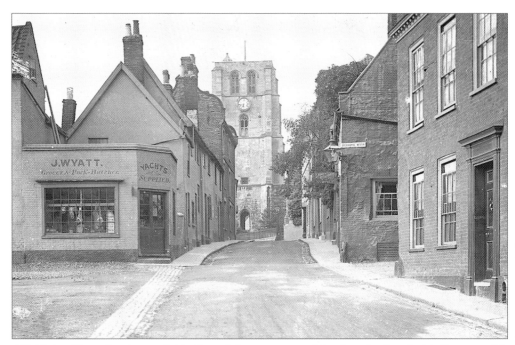

Old Market Place, Beccles, *c.* 1904. One of the curiosities of Beccles, the detached bell tower of St Michael's church, some 92 ft tall, is seen here at the top of Saltgate. A 1936 guide to the Broads gives this useless insight: 'The history of Beccles begins so long ago that there is no telling when'.

Northgate, Beccles, *c.* 1938. Still one of the most picturesque streets in Beccles, Northgate is now relatively peaceful thanks to a modern by-pass. In the distance can be seen the Number 17 bus on its regular run from Norwich to Lowestoft.

Broad View Studio and Tea Rooms, Bridge Road, Oulton Broad, *c.* 1910. On the extreme left is a poster advertising the latest attraction at Frank Rice's Burgh St Peter zoological gardens (which the poster calls 'an ideal spot'). Visitors are urged to take a trip on the River Waveney to see the 'sacred white camel'.

Main Street, Burgh Castle, *c.* 1913. This view shows the post office and the Queen's Head public house. The postmistress was Mrs Taylor and the landlord was Henry Bush. There were at least eight market gardeners trading in the parish at the time, an activity which has virtually disappeared now.

Coltishall village, August 1912. Such extensive damage to the heart of the village was the result of the collapse of the lock upstream at Buxton, which unleashed a surge of storm water, also wrecking the road bridge over the River Bure.

Wroxham village, c. 1935. Looking north from Wroxham Bridge, this view shows the growth of little shops and display boards which still dominate this area: the main Roys store is also visible in the distance. The coach is service G to London via Newmarket: passengers' suitcases were carried on top of the bus in a special rack.

Ranworth post office, 1935. Mr J.R. Neave's shop sold groceries, tobacco and milk for holiday-makers, as well as serving as the village post office. Displays in the window offer Lyons Tea and Cakes, Brasso, Zebo Easy Quick Clean and Kodak film.

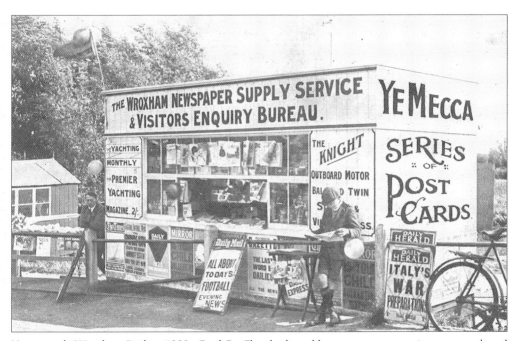

News stand, Wroxham Bridge, 1923. Cecil R. Chamberlin sold newspapers, magazines, postcards and souvenir guides – including in later years, his own. His first 'Chamberlin's Guide To The Broads' came out in May 1926, a fascinating period piece which even had a brief article on 'The Question of Provisions' by Arnold Roy, the entrepreneur behind Roys of Wroxham.

High Street, Stalham, *c.* 1914. From the number of children in their best clothes in this photograph, there is an air of preparation for a special event. On the right is Mrs Cattermoul's shop: at the time it was the post office, as well as being a stationer's, drapery and hosiery store.

Chapel Corner, Stalham, *c.* 1914. Less leafy now and with two absurd mini-roundabouts, this corner is still recognizable. The property behind the signpost was the wheelwright's/smith's: as so often this later became a garage and filling station. The Baptist chapel on the left was built in 1884 at a cost of £2,000.

Stalham Market, *c.* 1937. Although there is still a weekly Tuesday market on this site, it no longer offers such a full range of livestock and produce. The firm of Jonathan Howlett still runs 'Stalham Sale' as it is known locally, although its official title at the time was the East Norfolk Stock Mart.

Stalham High Street, *c.* 1910. On the left-hand side is the grand entrance to what is now Barclays Bank and further along is the awning of Hensman's Supply Stores (now Gateway). Hensman issued a catalogue of provisions for local delivery and for boating parties: an 1897 edition lists caviare at 1*s* 10*d* for a half-crown tin for cash customers.

Catfield Mill, *c*. 1934. This post mill was demolished in October 1937 and all that remains now is a circle of brick marking the foundations of the round house. Built in 1770, the sails and fantail were destroyed by a gale in 1926.

The Street, Catfield, 1910. These houses in the middle of Catfield village still survive, although are much altered: the one on the left is known as Threeways House. Unfortunately no details have been recorded of the identity of the ladies standing in the doorways.

Sutton post office, *c.* 1914. Mr Thomas Goodwin's post office, drapery and grocery store in Yarmouth Road was the main village shop at the time, but there was another shop, owned by Mr Edward Beales, as well as a boot maker, a basket maker and two inns – The Windmill and The Catherine Wheel.

West Somerton Stores, *c.* 1935. The postmaster in this village, Mr Charles Robert Pitchers, was not the only shopkeeper in West Somerton – Mr Charles Symonds ran another store nearby, in a parish of only 212 people!

Potter Heigham station, *c.* 1925. The Midland and Great Northern Railway came to Potter Heigham in January 1880. At first the trains could only take passengers as far as Yarmouth, but later the line was completed via North Walsham and Melton Constable to the Midlands. The station and the line closed in 1959.

Eastern Counties service 5 leaving Yarmouth Market Place, *c.* 1954. This Bristol L-type vehicle, with an Eastern Coach Works body, was a familiar sight throughout East Anglia until finally withdrawn in 1968. The No. 5 service took a long route from Norwich to Yarmouth to serve the main villages of the northern Broads; the fares did not rise once in the thirty years to 1950 and the full journey took 1¼ hours.

Bridge Stores, Potter Heigham, *c.* 1938. Gerrards' shop, just north of the bridge, boasted 'Everything needed is stocked'. It also offered full cooked meals in the restaurant, which held 'Jolly dances' with a first-class band throughout the summer season. Next door was the Potter Heigham branch of Roys and across the road was Broads-Haven stores.

'Top Shop', Potter Heigham, *c.* 1920. Mr James Watts' drapery and general store was some distance from the river and depended rather more on villagers than holiday-makers. Note the handcart for local deliveries, extreme right.

Thatched cottage, Hill Common, Hickling, *c.* 1908. This cottage still stands but it has been extended and modernized so that it is almost unrecognizable. The small community at Hill Common included eel fishers, boat men and reed cutters – all with a splendid view southwards across Hickling Broad. This photograph was used as a Christmas card from the owner, Laura Edgell; presumably it is her at the garden gate.

Uptown, Hickling, *c.* 1914. Hickling was, and is, a large parish with several distinct hamlets: Uptown, or Town Street, was a collection of thatched cottages clustered near to St Mary's Church and Hickling Hall.

Lower Street, Horning, *c*. 1927. The shop in the foreground is Gillard's Stores, but only a few years later it became the Horning branch of Roys – 'the local branch of the largest village store in the world'. Just beyond it occupying buildings on both sides of the road is Delves' Garage, itself a branch of a Norwich firm.

Post office, Horning, *c*. 1912. Albert Henry Cole served the village as postmaster from his grocery and general store in Lower Street. Next door can be seen Benjamin Sims' shop, also selling groceries, but famous for the 'Horning Bread' baked in brick ovens on the premises.

Filby post office, 1912. This shows the corner shop belonging to Walter S. English. A prominent notice-board on the gable points to the Filby Villa Tea Gardens, 'NB Closed on Sundays'.

Martham village centre, 1932. Many of the buildings seen in this photograph have survived, as has the pond, but the low cluster of buildings, centre left, has been demolished to make way for a Co-op supermarket.

Martham, 1909. This photograph of the village centre shows Clowes stores, a branch of a drapery and general merchant's in Yarmouth, and a cluster of old barns at the entrance to White Street which leads to the church. Note the thatched cottages on the right.

Martham, c. 1929. The barns remain, but the thatched cottages have now been swept away to make way for Mr Samuel Francis' new garage showroom. It is just possible to see some fine new black cars through the windows, although no details are visible, but Mr Francis was the authorized agent for Standard and Trojan cars.

Acle village centre, 1914. The Queen's Head, on the left, displays the shield of the Cyclists' Touring Club on the enormous gantry which supports its own inn sign. Cycling holidays were a popular and practical way of exploring the Broads district. The landlord at the time was Mr Samuel Richmond.

Damgate, Acle, 1914. Another of Acle's public houses, the King William IV, is shown here. It has long since gone, as has the brewery which supplied it, Steward and Patteson's of Norwich.

Acle Mill, *c.* 1914. The windmill had already lost a pair of sails and by this time all the work was powered by steam. It was owned by Wroxham Mills Ltd, although the building itself was undoubtedly the work of the Acle firm of Thomas Smithdale and Sons. This firm made boilers, scoop wheels, pumps, and erected steam mills, watermills and windmills.

Ludham village centre, *c.* 1930. Taken from the corner of the King's Arms public house, this view shows two shops and the shopkeepers. On the left is Powell's Stores, previously Lyon's, and next door is C.W. Clarke's general store.

Ludham village centre, *c.* 1948. Another view of Ludham Street, this time looking northwards. Again Powell's Stores can be seen, and next door is the entrance to Newtons – corn, flour, cereal and coal merchants. This building had earlier been a public house – The Baker's Arms. In the distance, Thrower's Stores can be seen, still flourishing today.

Norwich Road, Ludham, *c.* 1937. This view shows that there is a distinct hill towards the centre of Ludham, something which is scarcely detectable now that this delightful country lane has become the A1062 main road.

CHAPTER SEVEN

AND FINALLY . . .

Sutton Mill, the tallest in England.

So now the enchanted holiday is o'er.
Only from memory's page can men restore
The dear dead hours of yesterday, and soon
In vain we crave for memory's fleeting boon;
The morning and the evening are as one,
Night comes, and all is said, and all is done.
If for a little while my halting rhyme
Serve to remind you of this wondrous time
Of love renewed, and terror cast away,
'Twill not be penned in vain.
                                I've said my say;
Children, to bed; put out the cabin light,
God bless you every one, Good night, Good night.

Hugh Money-Coutts, 'The Broads 1919'.

Her Majesty safely moored after a successful launch, 1950. In December 1949 Broads Tours Ltd of Wroxham contracted with Herbert Woods Ltd of Potter Heigham to build and launch a 60 ft passenger vessel. The specification was for English oak for the hull, floor, stem and stern, with mahogany for much of the planking. The contract price was £3,500, to include a Morris engine.

Some of those who built *Her Majesty* at Herbert Woods' yard at Potter Heigham, 1950. Celebratory half-pints of beer all round was the order: little did these craftsmen realize that their skills would be superseded as the yards rapidly went over to glass fibre technology over the next decade or so.

Owner and builder of *Her Majesty*. The vessel was launched on time but there were some price increases in materials (controlled at that time by the government) and some extras, not least the costs of the launch party. The extra bill came to £801 11*s*, or as the invoice has it 'Say £800'. The picture shows Mr C.A. Hannaford of Broads Tours (left) and Mr Herbert Woods celebrating the launch.

Guests at the launch party. Among the guests are Mr and Mrs George Formby, Broads enthusiasts with a home at Wroxham (Heronby): note the splendid collars of his open-necked shirt. *Her Majesty* was launched by Lady Delia Peel and her first skipper was J.F. 'Dixie' Dean.

Motor Launch 1306, Potter Heigham, 1943. During the war the Woods yard was busier than ever with contracts for the Admiralty and the Ministry of Supply. The yard built sixteen of these launches (this was the last) for Coastal Convoy Escort patrols. To get them to the sea the superstructure was removed to allow passage under Acle Bridge, then reinstated in Yarmouth Harbour.

Breydon Viaduct, *c*. 1948. This was the greatest engineering feat on the Midland and Great Northern Joint Railway. It was opened in July 1903, the first rail link between Yarmouth and Lowestoft; it took nearly a year to demolish in 1962.

Breydon, February 1953. The most destructive tidal surge of modern times wreaked havoc on the last night of January 1953. This was the scene at the north wall of Breydon Water as water continued to pour across the railway into farmland. The picture was taken, at some risk, by Mr Bert Nichols, and loaned by his widow.

Breydon, February 1953. Another dramatic scene taken as the Breydon wall is breached and water cascades across the grazing lands near Breydon Junction signal box. This picture was also taken by Mr Nichols.

Martham Ferry, August 1912. This unusual picture shows Martham boat dyke in the foreground leading to the River Thurne. The old Martham ferry is partly adrift from its moorings, but the water is already going down and there was no permanent damage here. Note the very small buildings which are now the site of Martham Ferry boatyard.

Horning Ferry, *c.* 1920. There were really two ferries at Horning – the chain ferry for vehicles and an open punt for foot passengers, both operated by the same man; the villagers called him 'Clinks' from the noises of the chain. (*See also* p. 3).

Reedham Ferry, *c.* 1946. Not long after this photograph was taken the ferryman's lot was improved by the addition of an engine to haul the chain mechanism. Reedham Ferry – or Norton Ferry if you came from south of the river – is the last of the Broadland chain ferries still operating.

Gunner and houseboat, Breydon North Wall, *c.* 1949. There were several of these wooden shacks and huts, mostly based on boats but not actually afloat, for gunners and birdwatchers at Breydon: this one belonged to Harry Smith, although the man in the picture is unknown. The little wooden colony was swept away by the 1953 floods.

Reed lighter, Ranworth, April 1943. These traditional shallow-draught boats were a common sight on the Broads until quite recently. They were used by the marshmen to carry out reed, sedge and marsh hay; they could be navigated in the shallowest of marsh dykes and be rowed from either end – the middle was kept clear for the cargo – or quanted. This lighter was 23 ft by 7 ft, a typical example.

Wayford Bridge drainage windmill, *c.* 1912. This small mill demonstrates most of the features of the final development of Broads mills – a fantail to turn the sails to wind, patent sails (like louvres) controlled by a central 'spider', and a boat-shaped cap.

Hickling Broad, January 1929. Arctic winters are an occasional feature of the Broads and indeed in the days when the water was purer winter ice gathering was an important activity. Sleigh rides and ice-yachting enlivened this particular winter.

Hickling Broad, January 1929. The Broad was frozen solid and snow covered, poor for skating but worth removing sails from dinghies for use on this pair of ice yachts. The East Anglian climate still had the last word – it was too calm to make much headway.

ACKNOWLEDGEMENTS

I little thought when I started to compile *The Norfolk Broads In Old Photographs* that I should have the opportunity to put together this second selection, *Back To The Broads*. Fortunately, my own Broads collection was big and varied enough to withstand a further trawl for photographs and most of the pictures have come from that source. Nonetheless I could not have completed this book without very real help from many people, in particular Peter Bower, Di Cornell, Colin Cross, Mike Fuller, John Gilburt, Bertie High, Dorothy Hunt, James Hoseason, Arthur Lark, Ruth Knight, Shauna McDougall, Jennifer Mack, Pat Maitland, Bob Malster, Audrey Nichols, Simon Partridge, Stuart Press, Joan and Ken Saul, Jess Tunstall, and Joan Waters. I am also pleased to acknowledge my gratitude to Broads Tours of The Bridge, Wroxham, to The Filby Society, to Hoseasons Holidays of Sunway House, Raglan Road, Lowestoft, and to Wherry Yacht Charter of Barton House, Hartwell Road, Wroxham. The people and organizations named have loaned precious photographs and have generously given information, assistance and time. Humphrey Boardman lent his family albums to me, and it was a great sadness to hear of his death just as this book was going to press: my thanks and best wishes go to his daughter Shirley Place and his widow Isabel.

The poems which introduce each section come from the following sources. 'The Norfolk Wherry' is from *The Country Scene*, by John Masefield and Edward Seago, published by Collins, London, 1937. 'The Wood' was written by Martin Dring when he was a pupil of Hethersett Middle School, fresh from a stay at How Hill. 'To Suffolk', by Charles H. Lay, FRIBA, appeared in *Contemporary East Anglian Poetry*, published by Fowler Wright, London, 1928. 'The Rubaiyát of Potter Heigham', by 'Tolly', was a privately published verse account of a Broads cruise in August 1911, published in Leicester. 'Lines By An Exile', by Jeffrey Sorenson, appeared in the *Norfolk Magazine* in spring 1954. 'Suffolk', by Herbert Hudson, was included in *The Stewardship and Other Verses*, published in Ipswich, 1927. The final extract is taken from 'The Broads 1919', by Hugh Money-Coutts, published by John Lane, The Bodley Head, London, in 1920 – another verse account of a cruise, undertaken immediately after the horrors of the First World War.

I should also like to thank my wife Sue for her support and, as ever, for faultless typing. I have gone to great lengths to ensure that the information given is accurate, but sometimes the only source is my declining memory. Last time it was a great pleasure to receive kind letters giving corrected information or further details: please let me know if you find something amiss.

David Holmes
How Hill

SUTTON'S PHOTOGRAPHIC HISTORY OF TRANSPORT